MIXING WITH A DIVINE PURPOSE

A Call to Kingdom DJs

Jean Ndinsil (aka DJ LolaMax)

Contact: jan0707@yahoo.com

ISBN: 978-1-0674277-0-2

First edition 2026

Legal Deposit - Library and Archives Canada
Printed in Canada

DEDICATION

To the King of Kings, my Lord and Savior, Jesus Christ, the inspiration behind every beat and tune that fills my soul. May each note I play bring honor to Your name.

To my wife and children, who support me, carry me in prayer, and remind me every day that serving God is a privilege. May this book be a blessing to you and a testimony of God's faithfulness.

And to all DJs who have heard the call to serve the Kingdom, may this book guide you to mix not for fame, but for divine purposes.

PREFACE

There was a time when I believed DJing was only about lights, energy, and entertainment. Like many others, I saw the DJ booth as a stage, a place to shine. But when I started DJing just for fun in 2018, the more time I spent practicing, the more I realized that DJing could be used not only to enjoy music, but to truly offer praise to Jesus, my Saviour. I understood that the DJ booth could become an altar.

Through this revelation, I learned that DJing could be a ministry: a way to worship, to preach through sound, and to bring people into the presence of God. I also realized that many Christian DJs were still caught between two worlds. They had changed the songs they played, but not the mindset behind the mix.

That is why I wrote what is, to my knowledge, the first Christian book on the topic of DJing: *Mixing With a Divine Purpose*. This book is not about fame, lights, or technique. It is about consecration. It is a journey from being a Christian DJ to becoming a Kingdom DJ, one whose heart beats for the King and whose music releases Heaven on Earth.

My prayer is that as you read these pages, you will hear God's call: a call to serve, to worship, and to mix with divine purpose. May this book ignite something new in you. May you become a vessel through which Heaven's sound is released. And may your gift glorify Jesus Christ forever.

Jean Ndinsil (DJ LolaMax) Founder of **Kingdom DJ Academy**

ACKNOWLEDGMENTS

I want to thank my Lord and Savior Jesus Christ for saving me and transforming me. He has given me the incredible opportunity to serve Him through music.

To my family, thank you for your love, patience, and support throughout this journey. You are part of every beat that carries my message.

I want to thank every pastor, mentor, and friend who believed in this gift and has prayed for me, encouraged me, and shared their wisdom with me. I am forever grateful for your support and guidance.

To every Kingdom DJ, musician, worshipper and creative artist who desires to serve God with purity and excellence. This book was written because your ministry matters to God.

Thank you for opening your heart and allowing these words to speak to you. I pray that this book becomes a turning point, a confirmation, a calling and a strength for your journey as a servant of God.

May the Lord bless you and keep you. May your gift honor Him. May your life glorify Him. May your sound carry His presence.

Amen.

CONTENTS

A NECESSARY CLARIFICATION

This book was not written to teach DJing techniques. You will not find lessons on *beatmatching, transitions,* effects, controllers, or software. That choice is intentional. My primary concern is not the hands of the DJ, but the heart that guides those hands.

In the Kingdom of God, God always looks at the heart before He looks at the skill. Technique can impress people, but only a transformed heart can honor God. Jesus himself said that the Father is seeking *true worshippers* who worship Him in spirit and in truth (John 4:23). Being true begins in the heart long before it is expressed through sound.

This book was written to prepare the inner man before the outer work. Before God entrusts us with influence, He forms our identity. Before He uses our hands, He shapes our hearts.

Many DJs who come to Christ believe that serving God simply means changing their playlist. They stop playing secular music and start playing Christian songs. While this is a necessary step, it is not enough. When they were playing in clubs, everything was centered on technique, image, self-expression and audience approval. But when we serve God, everything must be centered on His glory and the edification of His people.

Serving God requires a different mindset. Jesus said, "Didn't you know I had to be in my Father's house?" (Luke 2:49).

This statement reveals Kingdom identity. A Kingdom DJ does not merely play Christian music. He identifies with the interests, priorities, and business of the Father. He sees himself first as a servant of the Kingdom, not as an artist seeking recognition.

A DJ can play Christian music and still not be aligned with God's heart. A DJ can say "Lord" with his lips and still serve himself in his motives. That is why the real work must happen in the heart.

This book is written to transform mindsets and prepare the heart of the Kingdom DJ. It is written to form servants, not performers. It is written to raise Kingdom agents, not religious entertainers.

The technique is important, but it must come after consecration. Skill is powerful, but only when guided by surrender. Hands are effective only when led by a heart fully devoted to God.

INTRODUCTION

When Solomon finished building the Temple of the Lord, a powerful moment unfolded. Scripture tells us that the priests consecrated themselves, the musicians took their place, and the singers lifted their voices together as one. Cymbals, harps, trumpets, and songs of praise rose toward Heaven. They were not performing for an audience. They were ministering before God.

Then something extraordinary happened.

"The Temple of the Lord was filled with the cloud, and the priests could not perform their service because of the cloud, for the glory of the Lord filled the house of God" (2 Chronicles 5:13-14).

God responded to consecrated worship with His manifest presence. The glory of the Lord filled the Temple so powerfully that human service had to stop. When God's glory arrived, human effort became secondary. Heaven took over.

This text reveals a timeless truth. When God's servants are set apart, united in purpose, and fully devoted to His glory, God reveals himself. Instruments become holy. Sound becomes sacred. Worship becomes encounter.

This is the vision behind this book. Just as the priests and musicians were consecrated for God's service, Kingdom DJs are called to a similar level of dedication. This book is not about entertainment. It is about consecration. It is about setting apart the heart, the hands, and the instruments for the glory of God.

Today, DJs hold tools different from harps and trumpets. Controllers, turntables, mixers, and software have replaced ancient instruments. Yet the principle has not changed. God still responds to worship that flows from a pure heart. He still fills the place where His glory is honored above all else.

This book was written to guide DJs into that mindset. To help them understand that mixing for God is not just about playing Christian songs, but about becoming a consecrated servant. When the heart is set apart, the sound carries weight. When life is holy, the atmosphere changes.

My prayer is that as you read these pages, you will be drawn into deeper consecration. That you will learn to approach your DJ booth as an altar. That your music will no longer be just sound, but a vessel through which God's glory can be revealed.

Why We Mix

When people hear the word DJ, most imagine flashing lights, wild crowds, smoke, and noise. For years, I did too. To me, DJing was about energy, attention, and applause. The DJ was the star of the night, the one who decided how people felt, moved, and remembered the event. But as I grew up in Christ, something inside me began to change. I started to sense that music, this gift I had loved since childhood, was not meant only to entertain. It was meant to minister.

I realized that behind every rhythm there is a spirit, and that every sound releases something, either light or darkness.

When a DJ stands behind the decks, he or she is not simply mixing tracks. They shape an atmosphere. That realization humbled me. I saw that I could either echo the culture of the world or host the presence of God. I could make people shout for excitement or lift their hands in worship.

That is when I began to pray differently:

"Lord, teach me to mix for You. Let every beat, every drop, every transition carry Your presence."

The Problem

The modern DJ scene celebrates fame, but rarely purpose. It exalts talent, but often ignores character. The decks have become stages of self-promotion rather than altars of surrender. Even among believers, many of us entered DJing with the same mentality the world taught us: to impress, to compete, to prove something.

But when Jesus becomes Lord of our craft, everything changes. We learn that God, not the crowd, is our first audience. We begin to understand that the purpose of our art is not applause, but adoration.

The Call

I believe we are standing in a new season for Christian DJs. God is raising a generation who will mix with divine purpose, sons and daughters who see the booth as a place of ministry, not performance. We will no longer chase platforms. We will build altars. We will no longer copy the sound of the world. We will release the sound of heaven through rhythm, beat, and joy.

This calling is not only about music style. It is about heart posture. The same God who anointed David to play the harp in Saul's palace is still anointing musicians today. This time, some of them hold USB drives and controllers instead of harps. The anointing has not changed. Only the instruments have evolved.

When we surrender our decks to God, our mixes become prayers. Every transition can declare, "Your Kingdom come." Every drop can proclaim, "Jesus reigns." Every rhythm can call a lost soul back to the Father's heart.

The Vision

I wrote this book as a mentor and a fellow servant, not as a celebrity DJ. My desire is to see you. Yes, you become a vessel God can trust in this generation. You might already be skilled behind the decks, or you might just be starting out. Either way, if your heart beats for God, you are in the right place.

In the following chapters, we will explore what it truly means to mix for God's glory:

• How to keep your heart pure behind the decks.

• how to choose music that honors Him

• How to create atmospheres where the Holy Spirit moves

• How to see yourself not as a performer, but as a minister of sound

We will walk together from heart transformation to practical ministry so that your talent becomes a tool in God's hands.

May the places where you enjoy recreation be filled with the divine presence, as the Temple was in Solomon's time. May Heaven respond to your obedience. And may it be said of your ministry that when you mixed, the glory of the Lord filled the place.

This is the call of the Kingdom DJ.

Reflection Questions

1. Why do I really want to DJ?
2. Who is my true audience when I play?
3. What does "mixing with purpose" mean to me personally?

Prayer

Father, thank You for the gift of music and rhythm. Teach me to see DJing as worship, not performance. Purify my motives, and let every sound I release bring You glory. May my booth become Your altar and my mixes a fragrance that pleases You. In Jesus' name, amen.

This is why we mix. Not to be known, but to make Him known. Not to entertain, but to edify. Not to be stars, but to be servants. DJs after God's own heart.

Chapter 1

THE HEART BEHIND THE DECKS

David's music had power because David's heart had purity. Before he played for the king, he worshipped in the fields.

Before God can use your hands to move a crowd, He must first shape your heart to move Heaven. Every Christian DJ must understand this truth: what happens on stage is simply the echo of what happens in secret. The decks will always reflect your heart.

When your heart burns for God, your mix carries fire. When your heart is distracted, your set feels empty, no matter how technically perfect it sounds.

DJing Is a Spiritual Act

We often separate ministry from music, as if God only works through preachers and not producers. But when you stand behind your controller, you are not just starting a playlist. You are stewarding the atmosphere.

In 1 Samuel 16:23, we read that whenever the spirit of distress came upon Saul, David would take the harp and play. Then relief would come to Saul, and the evil spirit would leave him. That is atmospheric ministry. David did not preach. He played. Yet his playing carried the presence of God.

Now imagine what can happen when a DJ, filled with the same Spirit, mixes beats not for ego, but for God's glory. Every loop, every pad hits, and every transition becomes a weapon against darkness. The mix becomes a message.

But here is the truth: David's music had power because David's heart had purity. Before he played for the king, he worshipped in the fields. Before he performed for people, he ministered before God. That is where our ministry as DJs must begin, in the secret place.

The Secret Place: Your Real Stage

Many DJs spend hours preparing playlists, EQ settings, and transitions. That is good. But how much time do we spend preparing our spirit?

Jesus said, "When you pray, go into your room, close the door and pray to your Father, who is unseen" (Matthew 6:6). This is the real stage, the place where we learn to mix in the Spirit before we mix in front of an audience.

When I started taking this seriously, my sets changed. Not because my transitions became smoother, but because my presence became stronger. People began to sense something beyond music: peace, joy, and conviction. That is when I realized the booth can become a pulpit if the heart behind it is surrendered.

When the Heart Is Not Right

Let us be honest. It is possible to play Christian music and still have a worldly heart. You can say, "It is for God," while still craving attention, likes, and validation. That is the subtle trap of performance.

As DJs, we enjoy applause and recognition. It feels good when people shout our name or celebrate our skills. This becomes a real challenge for those who serve God: learning how to receive appreciation while giving all glory back to the Lord.

Lucifer himself is described as a musical being in Scripture (Ezekiel 28:13). He was designed to glorify God, but pride corrupted his purpose. He wanted the spotlight instead of the Source. That same temptation still whispers today, "Show them what you can do."

The moment our desire shifts from God's glory to self-glory, the anointing lifts. The music may still be loud. It may still be impressive. But it becomes empty. God does not anoint skill. He anoints surrender.

Character Over Skill

If God had to choose between a DJ who is gifted but prideful and one who is humble but still learning, He would choose the second. Humility attracts grace, and grace produces growth.

As Kingdom DJs, we must pursue purity before popularity, character before creativity, and submission before success. Our goal is not to be the most impressive DJ, but to be the most trusted by Heaven.

Romans 12:1 calls us to offer our bodies as living sacrifices, holy and pleasing to God. This is our true and proper worship. That includes our hands, our ears, our choices, and our playlists.

When you treat your booth as an altar, everything changes. You become sensitive to what pleases God, not the crowd. You begin to hear His whispers between transitions. You realize that every sound check is also a spiritual check.

Practical Keys for a Pure Heart

Here are a few principles that have guided me through my own journey.

1. Pray before you play. Do not touch your gear before you speak with God. Dedicate every session, every set, and every event to Him.
2. Stay accountable. Surround yourself with people who can speak truth into your life. Pride grows in isolation.
3. Guard your inputs. The music you consume in private will shape what flows out in public.
4. Worship privately. If worship only happens during performances, it is no longer worship. It becomes performance.

5. Remember your why. When the crowd cheers, whisper in your heart, "All glory belongs to You, Lord."

When God Finds a Pure-Hearted DJ

When God finds a DJ whose heart is fully His. He can trust that person with influence. That is when revival can break out through rhythm. That is when joy and deliverance flow through beats. That is when a dance floor becomes a place of encounter.

Scripture says, "The eyes of the Lord range throughout the earth to strengthen those whose hearts are fully committed to Him" (2 Chronicles 16:9). May His eyes rest on you.

Reflection Questions

1. What motivates me most when I DJ, God's presence or people's praise?
2. How often do I mix in prayer before I mix in public?
3. What areas of my heart still need full surrender to God?

Prayer

Lord Jesus, thank You for calling me into this ministry of sound. Search my heart and remove anything that does not please You. Teach me to serve and not shine, to love and not compete. May my heart remain pure, and may my booth always be Your altar. I give You my music, my skills, and my dreams. Use them for Your glory. Amen.

Chapter 2

THE BOOTH AS AN ALTAR

Your booth is not just your workspace. It is your place of worship. It is where you meet God and invite others to do the same.

When most people see a DJ booth, they think of flashing lights, loud speakers, and dancing crowds. But when a Kingdom DJ steps into that same booth, something far more sacred is happening. Heaven is watching.

Every time you stand behind your decks, you are standing at an altar, not a stage. The difference between the two is simple. On a stage, people perform to be seen. At an altar, servants minister to please God.

The booth is where worship rises, where spiritual battles are fought, and where the atmosphere of Heaven invades the room. It is not entertainment. It is ministry.

The Biblical Meaning of the Altar

In the Old Testament, altars were places of encounter and surrender. They were not built for show. They were built for sacrifice. No one went to the altar without something to offer, whether a lamb, a dove, or grain.

Today, we no longer bring animals. We bring ourselves. Scripture says, "Present your bodies as a living sacrifice" (Romans 12:1). Every time you step into the booth, you bring your offering: your skills, your obedience, your passion, and your time.

You are saying, "Lord, here is my mix. Here is my creativity. Here is my heart. Use it for Your glory."

That moment of surrender transforms your DJ table into something holy. It becomes a modern altar where sound becomes sacrifice.

From Sound to Sacrifice

In the natural world, a DJ mixes frequencies. In the spiritual world, a minister of sound mixes faith, passion, and purity.

When your motives are pure, every transition becomes worship. When your heart burns for God, every drop becomes a declaration. Your set becomes a sacrifice of praise, as Scripture says, "Through Jesus, therefore, let us continually offer to God a sacrifice of praise" (Hebrews 13:15).

There is something sacred about that. It means your booth is not just your workspace. It is your place of worship. It is where you meet God and invite others to do the same.

So, when you prepare your playlist, do not think like an entertainer. Think like a Levite. In the Bible, the Levites were not there to perform. They were there to maintain God's presence in the Temple. That is your calling too, to maintain an atmosphere where God feels at home.

The Shift From Performance to Presence

Let us be honest. When you start DJing, it is easy to crave applause. You want the crowd to feel your drop, to dance, to react. That is normal. We are human.

But something powerful happens when you let go of performance and choose presence. You begin to realize that true satisfaction is not found in the crowd's energy, but in God's smile.

There is nothing wrong with energy and joy. In fact, God loves it when His people dance. Scripture says, "Let them praise His name with dancing" (Psalm 149:3). But our motivation must change. We do not play for the crowd. We play for the King. The crowd may clap, but the King crowns.

When you see your booth as an altar, you stop asking, "Did they like my set?" and start asking, "Did God receive my worship?"

Consecrating Your Booth

Before a Levite ministered at the altar, the altar had to be consecrated. That means it was separated from common use and dedicated to God.

Do the same with your equipment. It is not just gear. It is your ministry tool, your instrument of worship.

Here is how I consecrate my setup before an event.

First, I lay my hands on my decks and pray, "Lord, use this for Your glory." Second, I dedicate the space to the Holy Spirit and say, "Let every sound glorify You." Third, I invite God's presence to take over and declare, "You are the real Master tonight."

You would be amazed how the atmosphere changes when you do that. People will dance, yes, but more than that, they will feel peace, joy, healing, and conviction. That is what happens when your booth becomes an altar. God shows up.

The Altar Mindset

To minister from the booth as an altar, you need a new mindset.

First, you are not entertaining. You are interceding. Each track can carry a message, a prayer, or a prophetic direction. You are shaping a spiritual atmosphere.

Second, you are not showing off. You are serving. Like Jesus, your goal is to wash feet, not to raise hands for your own glory.

Third, you are not performing. You are partnering. The Holy Spirit is your co-DJ. You bring the beats. He brings the breakthrough.

Fourth, you are not chasing trends. You are channeling truth. What matters is not what is viral, but what is valuable in God's eyes.

The Fire on the Altar

In Leviticus 6:12-13, God commanded, "The fire on the altar must be kept burning; it must not go out."

This fire represented His presence. It was lit by God Himself, and the priests were responsible for keeping it alive.

That is our calling as Kingdom DJs. The Holy Spirit lit the fire when we were saved. Now we must keep it burning every time we play. Do not let routine or fatigue kill your fire. Stay in prayer. Stay inspired. Stay pure. Because once the fire goes out, the mix becomes mechanical and the ministry loses its impact.

Practical Steps to Keep Your Booth Holy

Begin with worship, not warm-up. Before soundcheck, play a worship track and let your heart connect with God.

Avoid secular samples or worldly lyrics. Do not bring strange fire to God's altar, as warned in Leviticus 10:1. Keep it pure.

Pray for the event, not just the energy. Ask God what He wants to do, whether joy, healing, or deliverance, and design your set around that mission.

Invite the Holy Spirit during the set. Whisper during transitions, "Guide me, Lord." Sometimes He will lead you to switch songs or slow down. End with gratitude. After the event, thank God for using you. Leave the altar in reverence.

Reflection Questions

1. Do I see my booth as a stage or an altar?

2. Have I consecrated my equipment and my music to God?
3. What changes can I make to invite God's presence more deeply during my sets?

Prayer

Father, thank You for trusting me with this ministry of sound. I consecrate my booth, my decks, my music, and my motives to You. Let my mixes become sacrifices of praise. Fill every frequency with Your presence, and let Your fire never go out. Make my booth Your altar and my life Your Temple. In Jesus' name, amen.

Chapter 3

THE CALLING OF A KINGDOM DJ

As a Kingdom DJ, your calling is to reclaim sound for God's glory. Wherever you go, whether youth events, weddings, street festivals, or online streams...

There is a big difference between someone who chooses to DJ and someone who is called to DJ. One mixes to express self. The other mixes to reveal God. A Kingdom DJ does not simply play music. He or she answers a divine calling.

Before you ever touched a controller, God already saw you behind the decks. Before you played your first beat, He already heard the sound of worship you would release. You are not a coincidence. You are a calling in motion.

God Still Calls Artists

Throughout Scripture, God has always called artists to serve Him. He called Bezalel in Exodus 31 and filled him with the

Spirit of God, with wisdom, understanding, and all kinds of skills, so that he could create artistic designs for the tabernacle.

This same pattern continues today. God still calls and anoints creatives, musicians, producers, sound engineers, and DJs to build atmospheres where His glory can dwell.

So, when you sense that deep stirring inside you, that love for music, that passion for rhythm, that hunger to use your art for His Kingdom, do not ignore it. It is not just talent. It is calling.

What Makes It a Calling?

A calling is not what you do for God. It is what God does through you. It is His assignment in your life; the divine reason you exist in your generation.

Being a Kingdom DJ is not simply about learning transitions or BPMs. It is about responding to a higher invitation. God is asking, "Will you be my instrument in this generation? Will you carry my sound to the nations?"

Your calling as a Kingdom DJ includes several dimensions.

First, worship leading. You guide people into God's presence through rhythm and sound. Second, atmosphere shifting. You use music to prepare hearts for encounters. Third, Kingdom representing. You become light in a world that often glorifies darkness. Fourth, teaching and discipling: you train others to use music with integrity and purpose.

You are not just spinning songs. You are stewarding souls through the ministry of sound.

The Kingdom DNA

The term "Kingdom DJ" means more than "Christian DJ." A Christian DJ plays Christian songs. A Kingdom DJ carries a Kingdom mission.

A Christian DJ often focuses on the playlist. A Kingdom DJ focuses on the presence. A Christian DJ works for events. A Kingdom DJ ministers for eternal impact. A Christian DJ sees DJing as a skill. A Kingdom DJ sees DJing as calling and worship. A Christian DJ may seek the approval of people. A Kingdom DJ seeks the affirmation of Heaven.

That is why I use the expression Kingdom DJing. The goal is not simply to play Christian songs, but to manifest the King through every set.

From Hobby to Holy Assignment

For many DJs, music begins as a hobby. They love beats, energy, and crowds. But when God steps in, He sanctifies that passion.

Your passion is not wrong. It simply needs direction. God does not erase your love for music. He redeems it. He takes what once moved people to dance in the flesh and transforms it to move them in the Spirit.

Think of Moses. He grew up trained in Pharaoh's palace with leadership skills, education, and strategy. All of it was secular preparation. But one encounter at the burning bush transformed his abilities into calling.

That is what happens when a DJ encounters Jesus. Your decks become your burning bush. Your music becomes your mission.

The DJ as a Modern-Day Psalmist

The psalms are filled with calls to worship God with instruments and joy. Scripture says, "Praise Him with the tambourine and dancing, praise Him with the strings and flute" (Psalm 150:4).

David did not play for entertainment. He played with revelation. Every sound carried spiritual weight.

This is your model. As a Kingdom DJ, you are a modern psalmist. You express divine truths through rhythm, not only through lyrics. Your transitions can tell stories of redemption. Your drops can mirror the joy of salvation. Even silence between songs can become a moment for the Holy Spirit to whisper. When you understand this, every set becomes a psalm in motion.

The DJ as a Spiritual Warrior

Music has always been a weapon in God's hands. When Jehoshaphat went to battle in 2 Chronicles 20, he did not send soldiers first. He sent worshippers. As they sang, "Give thanks to the Lord, for His mercy endures forever," God defeated the enemy.

This is a prophetic image for your ministry. When you play faith-filled music, you are not entertaining. You are fighting. You are breaking chains of depression, rebellion, addiction, and pride. Your decks become an altar of victory where darkness loses its power.

Never underestimate your mix. It is not just sound. It is a spiritual strategy.

Called to Influence Culture

One of the greatest lies is that music belongs to the world. Music belongs to God. The enemy corrupted it, but the Creator designed it.

As a Kingdom DJ, your calling is to reclaim sound for God's glory. Wherever you go, whether youth events, weddings, street festivals, or online streams, you push back darkness and make space for the Kingdom.

God does not want His DJs hidden only inside churches. He wants them to shine in culture, showing that joy, rhythm, and holiness can coexist beautifully. You are part of a new wave of Kingdom artists revealing that worship can move with excellence and fire.

Recognizing the Call

How do you know that you are called?

First, you feel deep conviction. Even when you try to stop, the desire to serve God through music keeps returning. Second, you see transformation. Your sets bring peace, joy, or conviction to people. Third, you experience spiritual resistance. The enemy often fights hardest against those who are truly called. Fourth, you receive confirmation. Godly mentors and leaders recognize the grace of God on your life.

When these signs align, you can be sure that you are not just talented. You are chosen.

Reflection Questions

1. Do I see DJing as my personal ambition or as God's divine assignment?

2. Am I mixing for influence or for eternal impact?
3. How can I begin to use my platform to represent the Kingdom more boldly?

Prayer

Father in Heaven, thank You for calling me into this generation of Kingdom DJs. I surrender my dreams and talents to You. Use me as Your instrument to release sounds of victory, joy, and transformation. Let my decks become my pulpit, and let my beats carry Your message. Help me walk in holiness, humility, and power. In Jesus' name, amen.

Chapter 4

CONSECRATED FOR THE DECKS: THE HOLINESS OF A KINGDOM DJ

Holiness is not perfection but separation. It means being set apart for a divine purpose.

God's first commandment to those He calls to serve Him is to be holy. In the Old Testament, the Levites could not touch the sacred instruments of worship without being consecrated. They needed their hands cleansed and anointed. In the same way, a Kingdom DJ cannot touch the turntables, the controller, or the sound system without understanding that these are now sacred tools. Once they have committed themselves to God, they no longer belong to the world; they become vessels of worship.

Holiness is not perfection but separation. It means being *set apart* for a divine purpose. When a DJ dedicates his art to God, the booth transforms into an altar. Every cable, every pad, every beat becomes a tool through which the presence of God can be expressed. A Kingdom DJ is aware that when he mixes, Heaven is watching. Angels are listening. The Holy Spirit is ready to move through his obedience.

In the realm of secular DJing, the DJ booth is often a stage for ego, a focal point of attention and celebration. However, for a Kingdom DJ, the booth becomes a place of submission. Instead of saying: "Look at me," the heart says: "Lord, use me." The focus shifts from seeking personal glory to furthering God's dominion. This is the very essence of devotion, not about diminishing one's abilities or imagination, but rather about yielding control to the Master.

Jesus had the habit of praying very early in the morning. This was His way of submitting to God and allowing Himself to be used by God. To align himself with God, the DJ must dedicate himself entirely to carrying out God's will. As Jesus Christ came to Earth to fulfill God's plan, so too must the DJ submit to God's purpose. I call this selfless surrender "consecration" in this text. The DJ willingly submits to God's use, all for God's glory.

"Very early in the morning, while it was still dark, Jesus got up, left the house and went off to a solitary place, where he prayed." Mark 1:35

"For I have come down from heaven not to do my will but to do the will of him who sent me." John 6:38

Consecration always involves sacrifice. For many DJs coming from the secular scene, this process begins with letting go of music that glorifies sin or self. This may involve deleting an entire playlist that once represented your identity. It could also mean forgoing attendance at events that don't align with your beliefs. Submitting to God's will may seem like a loss, but it is, in fact, a cleansing process. God cannot fill what is already full of the world. He only anoints what is empty and available.

When Isaiah encountered God in the Temple, he cried out, "Woe is me, for I am unclean." (Isaiah 6:5) It was only after the angel touched his lips with a burning coal that he was ready to say, "Here I am, send me." (Isaiah 6:8) The same principle applies to Kingdom DJs. Before you can be entrusted with mixing for souls, let God's fire burn within your heart. The decks are not just for sound; they are for spiritual impact. When your heart burns with purity, your mixes carry the fire from heaven.

Holiness also influences the unseen habits of a Kingdom DJ. What you watch, what you listen to, and what you meditate on all influence your spiritual sound. If your secret life is polluted, your public ministry will be powerless. The most powerful sets are not just those that are technically perfect, but those that come from a pure spirit. When the audience senses that your focus is on Jesus and not yourself, the atmosphere changes. The presence of God becomes tangible.

Being consecrated, just like the priests in the Temple, is about protecting the sanctified space within your booth. You should strive to maintain the purity and integrity of your creative environment, ensuring that those you collaborate with share your awe and devotion to God. A true Kingdom DJ never compromises their artistic vision or spirituality for fame or fleeting trends.

Nehemiah, as he led the reconstruction of Jerusalem's walls, resisted the aid offered by his adversaries, Sanballat, Tobiah, and the rest. Nehemiah knew that they did not have God's glory at heart, but were instead pursuing their own interests. His commitment was entirely devoted to God's work and to His glory, unlike his adversaries, who wanted to get involved without true devotion. The Kingdom DJ must also carefully choose his partners, as he is consecrated to divine service, not just to the pleasure of music or to alliances that do not seek God's glory. (Nehemiah 2:20)

God isn't looking for the best-known DJs. He's looking for the most faithful. Once he finds a dedicated DJ, he can give them spiritual authority. David wasn't chosen because he played better than anyone else. His heart was pure. His harp carried the anointing that drove away evil spirits. Similarly, when your heart stays true, your music becomes a tool of liberation. You no longer mix for entertainment, but for transformation.

Finally, consecration leads to joy. There is no greater fulfillment than knowing that your art brings joy to the One who created you. The Kingdom DJ, who is set apart, walks in divine peace, assured that he is fulfilling a heavenly mission. The applause of men quickly fades, but the approval of God endures forever. As you prepare for your next set, keep in mind that holiness is not a limitation, but a precious gift. Holiness gives you access to the divine presence and protects you in spiritual warfare.

Reflection Questions

1. Have I fully committed my music, equipment, and skills to God?
2. What worldly attachments may hinder my consecration as a Kingdom DJ?
3. How can I make my booth an altar where God is honored every time I play?

Prayer

Lord, I surrender my hands, heart, and music to You. Purify me and make me Your vessel. Teach me to mix in holiness and humility. Let every sound I release carry Your presence. May I stand out for Your glory, Lord. Amen.

Chapter 5

ANOINTED TO MOVE ATMOSPHERES

Anointing is not automatic. It flows where intimacy is maintained. The more time you spend in God's presence, the stronger the anointing becomes.

Some sounds have the power to stir people's emotions, while others have the ability to move Heaven itself. A secular DJ can certainly get a crowd going, but a Kingdom DJ possesses a unique ability to impact the spiritual realm. The difference is not just in skill, rhythm, or song selection. It is in the anointing. The anointing is the divine power of God that transforms natural talent into supernatural influence. It is what makes your set more than music. It becomes a ministry.

In the Bible, every person chosen by God for a specific role was anointed first. Kings, prophets, and priests were all set apart by the pouring of oil, symbolizing the empowerment of the Holy Spirit. That same principle applies to the

Kingdom DJ. The decks are your altar, the oil is the Spirit, and your sound becomes the offering. Without the anointing, mixing remains entertainment. With the anointing, it becomes an encounter.

The anointing changes everything because it shifts the source of power. In secular spaces, DJs depend on energy, lighting, and hype to move people. But the Kingdom DJ relies on the presence of the Holy Spirit. When the Spirit flows through your mix, hearts are healed, chains are broken, and joy is restored. You are more than a performer; you become a vessel through which the Spirit flows and works its miracles. The same Spirit who empowered David's harp to deliver Saul from torment can flow through your mix to deliver modern souls from oppression.

Anointing does not happen automatically. Instead, it emerges from sustained intimacy with God. The more time you spend in God's presence, the stronger the anointing will become. Private devotion fuels public power. When you pray before mixing, when you ask the Holy Spirit to lead your playlist, you invite Heaven into your craft. A seemingly simple transition between songs can become a divine moment that touches someone's spirit. One anointed mix can have a greater impact than a thousand perfect transitions.

The anointing also teaches. Jesus referred to the Holy Spirit as a teacher. He can inspire your creativity and help you hear rhythms from heaven. A kingdom DJ who relies on the anointing does not fear the crowd because their confidence comes from a divine partnership, not human approval.

It is essential to guard the anointing. Samson's strength didn't fail because the Spirit was insufficient; rather, it was due to his neglectful heart. Many talented DJs lose their divine blessings when pride enters their lives. The more God uses you, the more you must stay humble. Do not confuse being used by God with being approved by God. Anointing is a gift, but holiness is a choice. Keep your motives pure and your altar clean.

A true anointing is often characterized by a transformation in the environment. When a Kingdom DJ mixes under divine inspiration, something happens in the room. Joy becomes spiritual, and dancing turns into worship. People begin to feel God's presence. The beat becomes a heartbeat from heaven. You are not controlling people, but rather working in harmony with the Spirit, aligning yourself with Heaven's rhythm.

Moses understood the importance of God's presence. He said, "If Your presence does not go with us, do not send us" (Exodus 33:15). That should be the cry of every Kingdom DJ before touching the decks. In the absence of His presence, sound is just noise. But when His presence fills the room, every note becomes sacred. The anointing does not make you better than others. It makes you more useful for God's purposes.

The goal of a Kingdom DJ is not fame, but a spiritual influence. True anointing transforms your role from entertainer to atmosphere shifter. When you play, you are preparing ground for the Word, for prayer, for healing, and for joy. Every set becomes a mission field. Every beat becomes a declaration that the Kingdom of God is here.

Reflection Questions

1. Do I lean more on my abilities or the divine blessing of the Holy Spirit?

2. How can I deepen my relationship with God to enhance my anointing?

3. Have I ever experienced a spiritual transformation while mixing? What was God teaching me in that moment?

Prayer

Holy Spirit, fill me again with Your anointing. May the melodies I create echo with your divine power. Teach me to mix with revelation, not just rhythm. Use my sets to change atmospheres and hearts. May every song I play bring Heaven closer to earth. In Jesus' name, amen.

Chapter 6

THE POWER OF WORSHIP THROUGH BEATS

...a Kingdom DJ who mixes under the leading of the Holy Spirit can bring peace where there is confusion, joy where there is heaviness...

Praise and worship have never been tied to specific musical instruments or tunes. It has always been about heart and intention. From the first drumbeat in an African village to the strings of David's harp, God has always received praise through sound. The form may change, but the purpose remains the same: to honor the Creator. Every beat, loop, and transition for the Kingdom DJ is designed to serve one purpose: worship.

In the secular world, beats are used to stimulate emotion, energy, and movement. They create moments of excitement, but rarely lead to transformation. Yet, in the hands of a consecrated DJ, these same rhythmic elements can become channels of spiritual expression. The difference lies in the source of inspiration. The world uses rhythm to excite the flesh. The Kingdom DJ uses rhythm to awaken the spirit.

When David played his harp before Saul, the music carried divine presence. Evil spirits fled (1 Samuel 16:23). That was not just musical talent. That was anointed worship. In the same way, a DJ operating under the guidance of the Holy Spirit can bring order to chaos, happiness to sadness, and harmony to discord. Every sound becomes a spiritual tool.

God delights in creativity. He is the author of sound itself. The book of psalms encourages us to praise Him with the timbrel and dance, praise Him with stringed instruments and flutes (Psalm 150:4). If David were alive today, perhaps he would say, "Praise Him with decks and samples, praise Him with loops and pads." The instruments may evolve, but the heart of worship remains the same: adoration and surrender. What matters to God is not how loud your music is, but how pure your worship is.

For the Kingdom DJ, worship begins long before pressing play. It starts in the secret place, when you pray, fast, and seek God for inspiration. True worship through beats is born in intimacy, not in the crowd. The most powerful sets come from DJs who have already worshiped privately. When they step behind the decks, they are not trying to create God's presence. They are releasing what they already carry.

The beauty of worship through beats is that it transcends language. Even someone who doesn't understand the lyrics can experience the presence of God through the rhythm. The Spirit of God does not need translation. He only needs a willing vessel. This is why the Kingdom DJ's mission is so powerful. You can reach places and people that a sermon might not reach. When your sound is consecrated, it becomes a universal expression of God's glory.

But worship through beats must remain centered on God's glory, not human reaction. Many DJs begin with good intentions but end up seeking applause instead of presence. The Kingdom DJ must always remember that the dance floor can become a sanctuary if the heart remains humble. You are not performing for the people. You are leading them to God. The goal is not to impress, but to invite the Holy Spirit to take control.

When the crowd starts dancing with joy, don't think only of entertainment. Think of it as a victory. Every time people move freely in God's presence, chains are being broken. Worship through beats is a weapon for spiritual warfare. The rhythm of Heaven carries authority. Remember when the walls of Jericho fell after the sound of trumpets. That same principle applies today. God still uses sound to bring down barriers.

The Kingdom DJ's role is to bring order, beauty, and glory through rhythm. Every drop, every fade, every transition can carry purpose. You are building spiritual atmospheres where God is welcomed and people are transformed. Your beats become prayer, your mixes become offerings, your performance becomes worship. The decks are your altar, and your skill is your sacrifice.

Reflection Questions

1. Do I see my DJing as worship or as a performance?

2. How can I prepare spiritually before mixing to release God's presence through my beats?
3. What can I do to keep my focus on God's glory and not on people's reactions?

Prayer

Father, thank You for giving me rhythm and sound. Teach me to worship You through every beat. Let my mixes become prayers that rise to heaven. May every transition carry Your anointing, and every drop releases joy. Use my sound to bring healing, freedom, and unity to Your people. All glory to You, Lord of the beats. Amen.

Chapter 7

FROM CHRISTIAN DJ TO KINGDOM DJ

A Kingdom DJ does not perform for an audience. He ministers to souls.

Many DJs who have given their lives to Christ keep the same mindset as when they were in the secular scene. They stop playing explicit songs, replace them with clean or positive tracks, and believe that this change alone makes their work holy. Yet in the Kingdom of God, transformation goes far beyond song selection. It begins in the heart and extends to the purpose behind every mix.

1. The Difference Between a Christian DJ and a Kingdom DJ

A Christian DJ is someone who acknowledges Christ and chooses to play music that honors Him. This is a good beginning. However, a Kingdom DJ takes it a step further. He or she sees DJing as a sacred ministry, not a personal performance. Each track, each transition, and each atmosphere is guided by the desire to exalt the King and expand his Kingdom.

The Christian DJ plays for God. The Kingdom DJ plays with God. One prioritizes moral righteousness, while the other emphasizes spiritual devotion. One seeks acceptance from Christians. The other seeks alignment with the King.

2. Vessels of Honor in God's House

Paul wrote:

"In a large house there are articles not only of gold and silver but also of wood and clay. Some are for special purposes and some for common use. Those who cleanse themselves from the latter will be instruments for special purposes, made holy, useful to the Master and prepared to do any good work." (2 Timothy 2:20-21)

This truth defines the difference between the ordinary and the consecrated. In God's house, everyone has access to grace, but not everyone chooses to be a vessel of honor. A Kingdom DJ understands this call to holiness. He desires to be set apart for the Master's highest purpose.

3. Personal Reflection:

My spiritual life shifted when I discovered the truth Paul preached about vessels. Since then, I have decided to aim for vessels of value, and to become a vessel consecrated for God's highest use. This revelation changed everything for me in terms of how I live and serve.

Another powerful moment came when I read Amos 5:23 and Matthew 15:8-9. I understood that God doesn't just enjoy songs that mention His name or performances that repeat "Lord, Lord." He looks at the heart behind the sound.

"Take away from Me the noise of your songs; I will not listen to the melody of your harps." (Amos 5:23) "These people honor Me with their lips, but their hearts are far from Me." (Matthew 15:8-9)

These verses pierced my heart. They taught me that my service must reflect my inner life. God is selective about both the quality of the music offered to Him and the purity of the servant offering it. Ever since, I have committed myself to being a Kingdom DJ, a role that requires dedication, devotion, and sincerity. For me, DJing is no longer about creating excitement but about cultivating the presence of God.

4. The Risk of Remaining Only a Christian DJ

Remaining at the stage of a Christian DJ is like Israel remaining in the wilderness after leaving Egypt. You're free from slavery, but you haven't yet reached the promised land. Many Christian DJs stay in this middle ground. They avoid worldly lyrics but still chase worldly admiration. Their sets may sound clean, but their hearts still seek applause rather than divine approval.

Jesus warned us about this subtle danger:

"Not everyone who says to Me, 'Lord, Lord,' will enter the kingdom of heaven, but only the one who does the will of My Father who is in heaven." (Matthew 7:21)

A Christian DJ plays music that speaks about God. A Kingdom DJ plays music that flows from fellowship with God. The difference is life-changing.

5. Kingdom Mindset: Serving the King

The Kingdom DJ understands that music is not neutral. Every sound carries influence. Just as David played the harp and the evil spirit left Saul (1 Samuel 16:23), the anointing of your mix can shift atmospheres, heal hearts, and draw people closer to Christ. This is not achieved by skill alone but by consecration.

Paul reminds us: "Whatever you do, do it all for the glory of God." (1 Corinthians 10:31)

Every gig becomes an altar of worship. Every playlist becomes a sermon. Every fade and every transition become a devotional prayer to the Almighty.

6. From Performance to Priesthood

A Kingdom DJ does not perform for an audience. He ministers to souls. He understands that his booth is his altar. His USB stick is filled not only with tracks but with spiritual fire. His role resembles that of the Levites, who were chosen to serve in the presence of God (Numbers 3:12-13).

When you shift from entertainer to priest, your music takes on an eternal value. People no longer just dance. They encounter God. The joy becomes holy. The celebration becomes worship.

7. A Call to Consecration

This chapter is not written to condemn but to invite. God is calling DJs who have received His grace to now embrace His Kingdom. He is seeking those willing to leave the comfort of being Christian DJs and step into the holy responsibility of being Kingdom DJs.

Paul's words echo this invitation:

"I urge you, brothers and sisters, in view of God's mercy, to offer your bodies as a living sacrifice, holy and pleasing to God. This is your true and proper worship." (Romans 12:1)

To mix with divine purpose is to live with divine purpose. The decks become your pulpit, and every beat becomes your offering to the King of Kings.

Reflection Questions

1. Do I see myself more as a Christian DJ or as a Kingdom DJ, and why?
2. Am I serving God with a consecrated heart or mainly with clean music?
3. What mindset from my past does God want me to surrender today?
4. How does understanding DJing as a Kingdom calling change the way I serve?

Prayer

Father in Heaven,

Thank You for calling me into Your Kingdom and entrusting me with the gift of music. I ask You to search my heart and remove every motive that does not honor You. I do not want to be only a Christian DJ. I desire to be a Kingdom DJ, consecrated and useful for Your glory.

Chapter 8

BUILDING A KINGDOM PLAYLIST

The purpose is not only to avoid worldly lyrics but to cultivate an atmosphere where Christ is central.

Every Kingdom DJ must understand that preparing a set is not only a creative act. It is a spiritual assignment.

When you build a playlist, you are not just arranging songs. You are preparing a message from Heaven, a journey that God will use to touch lives. Each song, tempo, and transition can carry prophetic meaning when it is inspired by the Holy Spirit.

1. Seek God Before You Select

Before you choose a single song, begin with prayer. Seek guidance from the Holy Spirit, inquiring about the message He desires to convey through your music. In the Bible, David never went to battle without first seeking guidance from the Lord (2 Samuel 5:19). The Kingdom DJ must follow the same principle and ask, "Lord, what do You want to release through this set?"

Some nights, God will lead you to joy and celebration. Other times, He may guide you into moments of repentance, reflection, or healing. Your responsibility is to listen, not to guess.

"In all your ways, acknowledge Him, and He will direct your paths." (Proverbs 3:6) "The steps of a good man are ordered by the Lord." (Psalm 37:23)

When you acknowledge God even in your creative preparation, your playlist becomes anointed. The Spirit takes control of the flow.

2. Choose Songs That Glorify God

A Kingdom DJ must ensure that every track reflects God's nature and truth. Songs that glorify sin, pride, or self cannot coexist in a holy atmosphere. Consider the command given to Israel: "You must not bring a detestable thing into your house" (Deuteronomy 7:26). In the same way, do not bring songs into your mix that defile the altar.

Ask yourself these questions:

• Does this song lift up Jesus or the artist?

• Does it bring joy or confusion to the listener?

• Does it carry a message aligned with Scripture?

"Whatever you do, do it all for the glory of God." (1 Corinthians 10:31) "Let the message of Christ dwell among you richly, singing to God with gratitude in your hearts." (Colossians 3:16)

The purpose is not only to avoid worldly lyrics but to cultivate an atmosphere where Christ is central.

3. Flow with the Spirit, Not with Trends

In the secular scene, DJs build sets based on trends and popularity. A Kingdom DJ, however, builds according to God's timing. Remember Jesus' words: "The Son can do nothing by himself; He does only what He sees the Father doing. " (John 5:19).

You may plan your set carefully, but always remain flexible. If the Holy Spirit leads you to change a song in the middle, you must obey. The night belongs to God, not to your playlist. The best sets are not always the most technical. They are the most obedient.

"For those who are led by the Spirit of God are the children of God." (Romans 8:14)

Master the art of discerning divine flow. Sometimes, one Spirit-led transition can open hearts more deeply than an entire hour of perfect mixing.

4. Understand the Spiritual Journey

Every set should have a spiritual direction. Think of your set as a journey that takes listeners from their current state to where God wants them to be. In the Old Testament, Israel's worship process began with thanksgiving, moved into praise, and then entered the holy place of worship.

"Enter His gates with thanksgiving and His courts with praise; give thanks to Him and bless His name. " (Psalm 100:4)

This is a divine order. You can apply it by starting your set with joyful songs that lift the spirit, then moving into deeper songs that stir reverence and intimacy. The goal is not emotional manipulation but spiritual progression, bringing people from the outer court into the Holy of Holies.

5. Guard the Message of Your Mix

Your set is a sermon in sound. Just as preachers choose their words carefully, Kingdom DJs must select their tracks wisely. The Apostle Paul wrote, "Faith comes by hearing" (Romans 10:17). The songs you play influence what people believe, even subconsciously. Every lyric you release carries spiritual consequences.

Before finalizing your set, pray: "Lord, let nothing in this mix grieve Your Spirit."

6. End with Glory

Every Kingdom event must end pointing to God, not to the DJ. Finish your set with gratitude and worship, not with applause-seeking transitions. When the focus stays on Jesus, the presence of God lingers even after the music stops.

"He must increase, but I must decrease." (John 3:30) "Not to us, Lord, not to us, but to Your name be the glory." (Psalm 115:1)

Let your closing moments invite reflection, joy, and thanksgiving. That is when you know it was not just a party. It was a move of God.

Reflection Questions

1. How often do I seek the Holy Spirit's direction before choosing songs?
2. Are there tracks in my playlist that I need to remove or replace with Kingdom-centered ones?
3. Do I build my playlist for the Spirit's flow or for the crowd's reaction?

Prayer

Lord Jesus, guide my heart and my playlists. Teach me to build sets that honor You and lead Your people closer to Your presence. Fill me with wisdom to choose songs that glorify You alone. Let every mix I prepare become a message of love, truth, and freedom. In all things, may Your Kingdom come and Your will be done. Amen.

Chapter 9

THE MINISTRY OF SOUND: HOW THE KINGDOM DJ SERVES SOULS

Ministry is not an excuse for mediocrity; it's a call to higher standards

---

Kingdom DJs don't just manipulate music; they shape atmospheres. Every sound released can heal, encourage, and draw hearts closer to God, or distract and divide. That is why DJing for the Kingdom is not an art form alone. It is a ministry.

1. The DJ as a Servant, not a Star

Jesus defined greatness in one sentence: "The greatest among you will be your servant" (Matthew 23:11). This is the foundation of the Kingdom DJ mindset. In secular culture, the DJ is the center of attention, the one everyone looks at, cheers for, and photographs. But in the Kingdom, the DJ fades so that Jesus can shine. The spotlight belongs to the King.

A Kingdom DJ enters the booth with humility. You are there to serve God's people through sound, not to seek personal applause. Like John the Baptist, your heart must say, "He must increase, but I must decrease" (John 3:30). Every transition and every selection become an act of love toward the audience and obedience toward God.

2. Serving God's People Through Sound

In Scripture, music often accompanied moments of divine service. When the prophets ministered, musicians played, and the Spirit of God moved. "While the harpist was playing, the hand of the Lord came on Elisha" (2 Kings 3:15, 2 Chronicles 5:11-14).
The Kingdom DJ stands in that same line of ministry. Just as the harpist prepared the hearts of people to receive from God, the DJ is called to do the same. Sometimes your set will soften hearts before a message. Other times it will ignite faith, healing, or joy. Your goal is not only to entertain the crowd but to serve their souls.

Before every event, ask God, "What do Your people need tonight?"

Do they need encouragement? Do they need to be reminded of Your love? Do they need deliverance or a breakthrough? Then build your musical journey accordingly. This is what distinguishes a minister of sound from a performer.

"Each one should use whatever gift he has received to serve others, faithfully administering God's grace in its various forms" (1 Peter 4:10).

Your mixes are not just sounds; they are expressions of divine grace, music that carries the power of God.

3. The Sound That Heals

The Bible shows how sound carries power. When David played his harp, Saul's tormenting spirit left him (1 Samuel 16:23). When Israel shouted with the sound of trumpets, Jericho's walls fell (Joshua 6:20). Sound was never neutral. It was always spiritual.

As a Kingdom DJ, your sound can bring peace to a troubled heart, joy to a weary soul, and freedom to someone trapped in sin. The frequencies of Heaven are restorative. However, to release such sounds, your heart must remain pure. Only then will you produce a clean sound.

"If anyone cleanses himself from what is dishonorable, he will be a vessel for honorable use, set apart as holy and useful to the Master" (2 Timothy 2:21). Stay in prayer. Keep your conscience clear. Let your booth become a healing space.

4. Music as a Prophetic Tool

Sometimes the Holy Spirit will use your sound to speak messages that words cannot express. This is the prophetic dimension of Kingdom DJing when your mix becomes a voice of God's heart. You may feel led to play a specific song that carries a message someone in the room desperately needs.

"The one who prophesies speaks to people for their strengthening, encouraging, and comfort" (1 Corinthians 14:3).

A prophetic DJ does not just play songs. He releases messages. The Spirit uses them to strengthen, encourage, and comfort through rhythm and melody. That is ministry.

5. The Responsibility of the Kingdom DJ

With spiritual power comes spiritual responsibility. Jesus said, “To whom much is given, much will be required” (Luke 12:48). As a Kingdom DJ, your vocation requires excellence, honesty, and self-discipline. Be punctual. Be prepared. Be spiritually ready. The same God who anoints you expects you to be professional and trustworthy. Ministry is not an excuse for mediocrity. It is a call to higher standards.

Your ministry also extends beyond the booth. Pay close attention to those who come to you after your performance. Pray with them. Listen to their testimonies. Some may approach you not only because they enjoyed your music, but also because the Holy Spirit used it to touch their hearts. When this happens, treat them with the same humility that you demonstrated while mixing.

One moment that stood out to me was after a wedding where I served as the DJ. A man came up, hugged me firmly, and told me how deeply he had been blessed by the way I play music.

“You truly praise God through your music,” he said. “This is the third time I have attended a wedding where you DJ, and every time I experience the same powerful feeling.”

Those words have remained with me. Even when I’m exhausted from performing or struggling to pack up, I make an effort to remain approachable and willing to listen to those who want to talk. I think it is important to take a moment to connect with people, whether someone needs encouragement or just wants to share how my ministry has touched them. For me, that is what serving through music is all about.

6. The Reward of Servanthood

Serving others may seem hidden, but God sees it all. Jesus promised, "Your Father, who sees what is done in secret, will reward you" (Matthew 6:4). When you serve faithfully, God opens doors of influence and anoints your sound with greater authority. The more you pour out, the more He fills you.

The Kingdom DJ does not serve for recognition. He serves for transformation. Every life changed, every soul uplifted, and every tear of gratitude are your eternal reward.

Reflection Questions

1. Do I see my DJing as ministry or performance?
2. How do I prepare spiritually to serve God's people through sound?
3. Am I willing to decrease so that Christ may increase through my art?

Prayer

Lord Jesus, thank You for the privilege of serving through music. Make me a faithful servant who ministers with love, humility, and excellence. Let every sound I release carry Your presence and bring healing to hearts. Teach me to see every event as an opportunity to serve Your Kingdom. May my booth always be Your altar, and my sound a tool for Your glory. Amen.

Chapter 10

EXCELLENCE AND SPIRITUAL DISCIPLINE: THE CHARACTER OF A KINGDOM DJ

Excellence reveals whom you serve. Mediocrity whispers that God isn't worth the effort

---

In the Kingdom of God, anointing without discipline is dangerous, and talent without character is empty. A Kingdom DJ is called not only to move crowds, but also to move heaven. To do this effectively, you must cultivate both spiritual depth and professional excellence.

Excellence is not pride. It is worship. When you give God your best, you honor Him. "Whatever you do, work at it with all your heart, as working for the Lord, not for men" (Colossians 3:23).

1. Excellence as Worship

Many think that excellence is about impressing people, but in the Kingdom, it is about honoring God. When Solomon built the Temple, he did not use leftover materials or ordinary craftsmanship. Everything was done with precision, beauty, and order because it was for the Lord (1 Kings 6:14-22).

In the same way, your DJ craft must reflect your reverence for God. Every mix, every set, and every sound choice should be done with intention and prayer. Excellence reveals whom you serve. Mediocrity whispers that God isn't worth the effort—but excellence proclaims His greatness.

Psalm 33:3 says, "Sing to Him a new song. Play skillfully and shout for joy."

Notice the words play skillfully. God expects skill in worship.

When you spend hours practicing transitions, refining your sound, or learning new gear, it is not vanity. Rather, it is a tangible sign of your devotion. It is your way of saying, "Lord, I will not offer You something that costs me nothing" (2 Samuel 24:24).

2. Spiritual Discipline: The Root of True Power

A Kingdom DJ cannot rely only on talent or energy. The power that transforms atmospheres comes from a secret place. Without prayer, your sound will remain natural. With prayer, your sound becomes supernatural.

Luke 5:16 says, "But Jesus often withdrew to lonely places and prayed." If even Jesus needed solitude to stay aligned with the Father, how much more do we?

Spiritual discipline is consistent prayer and meditation on the Word. The Holy Spirit fine-tunes your spirit just as you fine-tune frequencies. Without that alignment, your art becomes noise instead of ministry.

Here are key disciplines every Kingdom DJ should cultivate.

Daily prayer to stay connected to your Source. Bible study to fill your mind with truth and revelation. Silence and reflection to hear God's voice clearly. The more disciplined you are spiritually, the more authority your music will carry. People may not understand why your sets feel different, but the reason is simple: you have spent time with the King.

3. The Excellence of Character

Excellence is not just about what you do; it's also about who you are. It reflects humility, honesty, punctuality, and faithfulness. Jesus said, "Let your yes be yes and your no be no" (Matthew 5:37). A Kingdom DJ's word must be trustworthy.

In ministry, your reputation is as important as your sound. Your testimony speaks more powerfully than your mix. You cannot effectively spread life if your personal behavior contradicts your message. Integrity is the amplifier of your anointing.

Proverbs 22:1 says, "A good name is more desirable than great riches. To be esteemed is better than silver or gold."

Let your lifestyle, speech, and social media reflect the same holiness you express through music. When people see consistency between your art and your character, they will respect your ministry and be drawn to Christ.

4. Training the Hands and the Heart

David was both a warrior and a musician. He trained his hands for battle and his heart for worship.

Psalm 144:1 says: “Praise be to the Lord, who trains my hands for war, my fingers for battle.”

The Kingdom DJ also needs both trained hands and a trained heart. Your hands mix the sounds. Your heart directs the flow. Skills without sensitivity create a performance. Sensitivity without skill creates confusion. But when both are developed, Heaven and Earth meet in your sound.

Practice your craft diligently. Learn your equipment, understand your software, and rehearse transitions. At the same time, practice love, patience, humility, and self-control. That is how excellence becomes spiritual.

5. Accountability and Growth

No one grows up alone. Every true minister must be accountable to someone, a pastor, mentor, or spiritual leader.

Proverbs 27:17 says: “As iron sharpens iron, so one person sharpens another.”

Accountability protects your anointing. It keeps pride from creeping in. Allow others to offer you feedback and pray with you. The more you submit to godly leadership, the more authority God entrusts you with.

Also, seek constant learning. Read books on music, ministry, and leadership. Attend workshops. Stay teachable. Excellence is a lifelong pursuit.

6. Faithfulness in the Small Things

Jesus said: "Whoever can be trusted with very little can also be trusted with much" (Luke 16:10). If you cannot handle a small crowd with passion and excellence, you are not ready for a big one. God watches how you handle the hidden seasons. The excellence you show in private determines the public recognition you will receive.

Be faithful in rehearsals, faithful in your preparation, and faithful even when no one is watching. Heaven promotes servants, not stars.

7. The Reward of Excellence

God is pleased when you pursue excellence for His glory.

Matthew 25:21 says: "Well done, good and faithful servant. You have been faithful with a few things. I will put you in charge of many things. Come and share your master's happiness."

Every effort you put into refining your gift is an investment in eternity. The more you master your art, the more God can trust you to impact nations through it.

Reflection Questions

1. Am I giving God my best in both my art and my character?
2. How consistent is my spiritual discipline when no one sees me?
3. Do I see practice and preparation as part of my worship?

4. To whom am I responsible in my ministry?

Prayer

Lord, thank You for calling me to serve You through music. Teach me to pursue excellence, not for fame, but for Your glory. Discipline my spirit to seek You daily. Shape my character to reflect Your holiness. Train my hands for skill and my heart for humility. May all that I create bring glory to Your name and draw souls closer to You. In Jesus's name, amen.

Chapter 11

THE ANOINTING AND THE FLOW: PARTNERING WITH THE HOLY SPIRIT DURING A SET

True flow happens when the DJ and the Spirit move together in rhythm.

Every Kingdom DJ must understand this truth: the booth can become an altar when the Holy Spirit is present. Your gear is not simply a tool, but an instrument for worship. Your songs are not just sounds. They are vessels of glory. And your hands are not just mixing beats. They are releasing atmospheres.

The anointing is what separates a Kingdom DJ from every other performer. Without the Holy Spirit, even the most perfect mix remains ordinary. But when the Spirit flows, Heaven invades the room.

"Not by might nor by power, but by My Spirit," says the Lord Almighty (Zechariah 4:6).

1. Understanding the Anointing

The anointing is God's divine empowerment, enabling you to do what you could never do on your own. It is not emotional excitement or loud music. It is the tangible presence of God operating through you.

"The Spirit of the Sovereign Lord is upon me, because the Lord has anointed me to proclaim good news to the poor" (Isaiah 61:1).

When you're anointed, your mix becomes a message. The music you play carries healing, freedom, conviction, and joy. In the same way David's harp drove away the evil spirit from Saul (1 Samuel 16:23), your mixes can bring peace and restoration to hearts when the anointing flows.

2. Preparing the Vessel

Prior to God's flow through you, He must first purify you. Anointing finds its best expression in a pure vessel. You cannot expect Heaven's power to rest on a life that compromises with sin.

"If anyone cleanses himself from what is dishonorable, he will be a vessel for honorable use, set apart as holy, useful to the Master and prepared for every good work" (2 Timothy 2:21).

The time you spend in prayer before a set is not optional. It is essential. Ask the Holy Spirit to search your heart, remove pride, and fill you with His presence. Your preparation is not just technical. It is spiritual. The more consecrated you are, the more powerful your set becomes.

3. Creating Space for the Spirit

A Kingdom DJ does not control the Spirit; he follows Him. There will be moments during a set when you sense a shift. The crowd might suddenly become silent, or a particular song may evoke strong emotions. That is often the Holy Spirit moving. Avoid interrupting these moments. Follow His flow.

"The wind blows wherever it pleases. You hear its sound, but you cannot tell where it comes from or where it is going. So, it is with everyone born of the Spirit" (John 3:8).

Learn to read not only the crowd but also the atmosphere. Be sensitive to what Heaven is doing in the room. Sometimes, He may prompt you to slow down, play a worship song, or even stop completely for prayer. True flow happens when the DJ and the Spirit move together in rhythm.

4. When Heaven Takes Over

Sometimes, the Holy Spirit can completely take over a set, and you'll know it when the songs sync perfectly, hearts open, and the presence of God permeates the room. These are divine appointments. You are no longer the one mixing. God is.

"While they were worshiping the Lord and fasting, the Holy Spirit said…" (Acts 13:2).

Notice that while they were worshiping, the Spirit spoke. The same can happen through your mix. God can release prophetic direction, healing, or deliverance through the sound you play when your heart and hands are yielded.

Do not be afraid of silence, tears, or unusual moments. The Kingdom DJ isn't there to entertain. He's there to host God's presence.

5. Balancing Structure and Spontaneity

It is wise to prepare your playlist, but you must remain flexible. David prepared instruments, singers, and order for worship in the Temple (1 Chronicles 25:6-7), yet the Spirit still moved freely among them. Preparation gives you structure. Sensitivity gives you flow. Both are necessary.

Before each performance, seek divine guidance from God for the sequencing of your songs. As you mix, keep your spiritual ears open. If the Spirit shifts direction, follow immediately. That is when a supernatural impact happens.

6. Recognizing Spiritual Impact

The anointing leads to transformation. You will see people cry, kneel, dance with freedom, or remain still in awe. Some will experience inner healing. Others will receive deliverance. Do not seek these signs. Seek His presence, and they will come naturally.

"Where the Spirit of the Lord is, there is freedom" (2 Corinthians 3:17).

Music becomes a carrier of freedom. That is what separates a Kingdom DJ from a performer. The secular DJ moves emotions. The Kingdom DJ moves spirits.

7. Protecting the Anointing

The anointing is precious, but it can be lost through negligence or pride. Protect it with humility, integrity, and consistent intimacy with God. Remember that you are just a vessel, not the source of power.

"What do you have that you did not receive?" (1 Corinthians 4:7).

After each set, give glory back to God. Thank Him, pray again, and rest in His presence. Your goal is not to trend. Your goal is to please the King.

I remember returning from a wedding where I was DJing. During the event, I distinctly sensed the Spirit of God, prompting me to worship my Savior through the music. That night, I was overwhelmed with emotion. As I drove alone in my van at around 1 a.m., I spent the whole hour in worship. As Kingdom DJs, our greatest joy is when we mix with God's glory in mind.

8. Becoming a Conduit of Heaven

Imagine every set as a spiritual mission. You are the intermediary between Heaven and Earth. You have a role to play in releasing Heaven's sound into the world. When people leave your event, they should not just say, "The DJ was good." Instead, they should proclaim, "God was here."

"For the earth will be filled with the knowledge of the glory of the Lord as the waters cover the sea" (Habakkuk 2:14).

You are part of the fulfillment of that promise. Through your sound, the knowledge of God's glory spreads.

Reflection Questions

1. Do I take the time to pray and prepare spiritually before each mix?

2. Am I sensitive to the Holy Spirit's flow while mixing?
3. Have I learned to pause when Heaven is moving?
4. Do I give God the glory after every event?

Prayer

Holy Spirit, thank You for trusting me to serve You through music. Guide me to align with your flow, discern your voice, and follow your lead. Let every sound I release carry Your presence. Purify my heart, anoint my hands, and make me an instrument of Heaven on Earth. May every mix bring You glory and touch lives for eternity. In Jesus' name, amen.

CONCLUSION

A Christian DJ seeks to avoid what is sinful. A Kingdom DJ seeks to pursue what is holy.

You have now reached the end of this journey, but in truth, this is only the beginning. Throughout, the message has been clear: DJing for God is not a performance. It is a calling.

As you stand at the DJ booth, Heaven witnesses your every move. As you raise your hands to mix, you are not just manipulating sounds, but creating atmospheres. You have been chosen to serve the King of Kings with a gift that once graced the world. What an honor.

"Each of you should use whatever gift you have received to serve others, as faithful stewards of God's grace in its various forms, so that, in all things, God may be praised through Jesus Christ" (1 Peter 4:10-11).

The Kingdom DJ understands that everything begins and ends with God's glory. He is not the star. God is. He does not play to impress. He plays to express Heaven's heartbeat. He does not seek applause. He seeks the anointing.

Your gift was never meant to build your name. It was designed to lift His.

1. From the Booth to the Altar

You have learned throughout this book that the difference between a Christian DJ and a Kingdom DJ is not only in the songs they play, but in the spirit they carry. A Christian DJ tries to avoid sin. A Kingdom DJ seeks to pursue holiness. One plays clean. The other plays consecrated.

The booth becomes an altar when your motive becomes worship. You stop performing; you minister. You no longer mix for entertainment; you mix for edification. Every sound becomes a sacrifice of praise.

"Offer your bodies as a living sacrifice, holy and pleasing to God. This is your true and proper worship" (Romans 12:1).

When you step behind your console, remember that you are a priest in service. The lights, the beats, and the transitions can all be holy when your heart is fully surrendered.

2. Let the Kingdom Mindset Lead You

The Kingdom mindset is not about religion or style; it is about alignment with Heaven. Jesus taught us to pray, "Your Kingdom comes, Your will be done, on earth as it is in Heaven" (Matthew 6:10).

That is your mission as a Kingdom DJ, to bring the sound of Heaven down to Earth. Every mix can become a prayer. Every drop can become a proclamation. Every loop can become a revelation.

But this requires a heart governed by Kingdom principles: love, humility, holiness, and purpose. In the Kingdom, power flows through purity. The more you surrender, the more God can move through you.

"For the eyes of the Lord range throughout the earth to strengthen those whose hearts are fully committed to Him" (2 Chronicles 16:9).

Aim to be an exceptional DJ, a selfless servant with a fully devoted heart. Let the Spirit of God flow through your equipment, your creativity, and your passion.

3. Excellence, Consecration, and Flow

On this journey, never separate spirituality from skill. Both must grow together. Excellence honors God. Discipline protects the anointing. The Holy Spirit provides the flow.

You don't have to mimic the world to connect with it. Instead, aim to speak from Heaven. Remain unadulterated. Keep your thirst intact. Stay receptive to learning. Perfect your craft with dedication. Pray beforehand. Serve with humility.

"And David shepherded them with integrity of heart; with skillful hands he led them." (Psalm 78:72).

Let that verse define your ministry: integrity of heart and skillful hands.

4. The Next Chapter of Your Journey

Now that you know how to mix with a purpose, the next step is to live with a purpose. Every event, every song and every opportunity is a divine assignment. Ask God before every gig, "Lord, what do You want to do through me tonight?"

Sometimes He will use your mix to spark joy. Other times He will use it to bring healing, unity, or conviction. Be ready for anything, because when you carry the Kingdom, anything can happen.

“Then the disciples went out and preached everywhere, and the Lord worked with them and confirmed His word by the signs that accompanied it” (Mark 16:20).

As you mix, God will work with you. He will use your sound to confirm His Word in people’s hearts.

5. The Final Call

The Kingdom DJ movement is not just about music; it’s about revival. God is raising a generation of sound ministers who refuse to copy the world and are ready to transform it. Through your decks, God will touch lives you may never even meet.

So, guard your anointing. Cherish your congregation. Submit to your God-fearing leaders. Above all, remain rooted in the Source. Never allow the crowd’s applause to replace the voice of the Holy Spirit.

“Apart from Me, you can do nothing” (John 15:5).

Your strength lies in your relationship with God. Your power comes from purity. Your fruit stems from your faithfulness.

When you stand before Heaven one day, Jesus will not ask how many followers you had. He will ask how many hearts you served.

Final Exhortation

Turn your booth into an altar. Use your music as a tool for ministry. Allow your passion to become your prayer. Make your mix your message.

You are not just a DJ, but an ambassador of the Kingdom. The world has its own music, but heaven has its own, and God has entrusted you with the task of releasing it.

"For the earth will be filled with the knowledge of the glory of the Lord as the waters cover the sea" (Habakkuk 2:14).

Go now and fill the earth with that glory, one mix at a time.

PASTORAL NOTE

1. A Note to the Converted Secular DJ: From the Booth of Egypt to the Altar of the Kingdom

Welcome home! By devoting your heart and skills to Jesus Christ, you have taken a crucial step toward a new life. Heaven is filled with joy as yet another artist is saved from darkness and brought into the wonderful light of God's kingdom (1 Peter 2:9).

However, this transformation is more than just a shift in music. It's a transformation of mindset. Previously, your music catered to your emotions, enhanced your ego, and reflected the world's ambiance. Now you must serve the King with your music.

Before you start mixing for God, pause and allow Him to transform your heart. Ask yourself:

• What attracted me to DJing in the secular world?

• What did I seek when I stood behind the decks, fame, applause, money, pleasure, or influence?

• How did I prepare for each gig? Did I depend on energy drinks, alcohol, or substances to feel the vibe?

• How did I view the crowd, as souls or as fans?

These inquiries are not intended to judge you, but to prompt self-reflection. God doesn't want to employ your former self in a new role. He wants to make you a new creation.

"Do not conform to the pattern of this world, but be transformed by the renewing of your mind" (Romans 12:2).

You have left Egypt, but Egypt must also leave your heart. Israel required forty years in the desert to be cleansed from a mentality of servitude before entering the Promised Land. You, too, deserve a time of dedication. Avoid rushing back to your station. Let the Holy Spirit instruct you in a fresh tempo: the tempo of the Kingdom.

"If anyone is in Christ, he is a new creation; the old has gone, the new has come." (2 Corinthians 5:17).

Take time to grow under your pastor's mentorship. Study the Word, worship, and pray. Learn what it truly means to serve. This book is designed as a companion to help you do all these things with purpose and a renewed heart.

God wants more than just your talents. He wants your life. When your heart is pure, your hands will mix with divine intentions. The skills you have learned in the world will now serve heavenly purposes.

Keep in mind this truth: a Kingdom DJ is not just a musician who plays clean songs. He is a minister, a spiritual leader, standing behind the turntables. His booth transforms into a sacred space, and his performance becomes a worship offering.

2. A Note to the Christian DJ Influenced by the World: From Clean Sound to Consecrated Sound

Maybe you have been DJing in the church for years. You only play Christian music, avoiding profanity in the lyrics. However, you can't help but notice that your style, your motivations, and even your aspirations still reflect those of secular DJs. You follow the techniques of worldly DJs, mimic their stage presence, and sometimes envy their fame.

This is a dangerous mixture, a clean sound with a contaminated heart.

"Do you not know that friendship with the world means enmity against God?" (James 4:4).

God is calling you higher. He is calling you to become a Kingdom DJ, a consecrated servant rather than a Christian performer. This means your first desire is no longer to impress people, but to please God. Your ministry becomes holy when your mindset becomes Kingdom focused.

A Christian DJ plays good music. A Kingdom DJ hosts God's presence. That is the difference.

The Kingdom DJ understands that his set is a spiritual mission. He does not copy the patterns of the world; he receives direction from Heaven. His music becomes a tool of revival, and his life becomes an example of holiness.

"But just as He who called you is holy, so be holy in all you do; for it is written: 'Be holy because I am holy.'" (1 Peter 1:15-16).

You have already mastered the art. Now it's time to master your heart. Allow the Holy Spirit to purify your intentions.

Craft your playlist not based on popularity, but through prayer. Don't be afraid to be unique. Consecration always sets one apart.

You may lose some followers, but you will gain God's approval. You may not trend online, but you will receive Heaven's applause. And one day, when your mission is complete, you will hear the most beautiful words ever spoken:

"Well done, good and faithful servant" (Matthew 25:21).

That is the crown that every kingdom DJ must desire.

FINAL WORDS

As you reach the end of this book, I want to share my heart with you. I am more than a DJ, I am a servant of the Most High God, devoted to using the gift. He entrusted to me. Music is not mine to claim; it comes from the Creator of sound. Over the years, I've learned how deeply music touches the soul, and I've discovered the power of true praise. Scripture says that God inhabits the praises of His people, and that truth has transformed my purpose.

Today, nothing brings me greater joy than honoring God through music. When I stand behind my DJ console, it is a form of devotion. Every mix, every transition, and every beat is my way of praising the Lord. What others might perceive as entertainment, I consider a divine encounter, where heaven and earth connect through sound.

My DJ name, DJ LolaMax, reflects that calling. "Lola" means "Heaven" in Lingala, and "Max" means "Maximum." Together, they express my mission: to release Heaven's atmosphere to the fullest so God's people can praise Him with all their strength and joy.

I have always been driven to promote the Kingdom DJing movement, a group of dedicated DJs who mix not for personal glory, but for the glory of God. That passion led me to create **Kingdom DJ Academy**, an online platform dedicated to training Spirit-led DJs in both skill and purpose.

If this mission resonates with you, I cordially invite you to join our Academy. There, you will not only develop your skills as a DJ, but also deepen your spiritual understanding and calling. Together, we can raise a generation that brings revival through music.

Please don't hesitate to contact me. I would be honored to walk with you and see how God can use your gift for His glory. May the Lord bless you, fill you with His Spirit, and anoint your hands for His Kingdom. May every sound you release shine His light into the darkness.

Let every mix declare one truth: Jesus is Lord. With love and purpose,

Jean-Ndinsil (DJ LolaMax) Founder, *Kingdom DJ Academy*

ABOUT THE AUTHOR

DJ LolaMax is a Canadian artist, producer, author and educator who specializes in Christian music. He has always loved music, and at the age of 17, he encountered Christ and dedicated his creative gifts to the Lord. For many years, he worked as a worship leader and a youth pastor before discovering DJing as a powerful form of worship. Founder of the Kingdom DJ Academy, LolaMax trains and mentors new generations of DJs who want to use their talents to glorify God. His life's mission is clear: *to raise consecrated Kingdom DJs who mix with divine purpose.*

Connect with DJ LolaMax: **jan0707@yahoo.com**
youtube.com/@djlolamax | TikTok: DJ LolaMax

About Kingdom DJ Academy

Kingdom DJ Academy is a global movement raising consecrated DJs who mix for the glory of God. We equip artists spiritually and technically to bring revival through sound. Join the new generation of Kingdom DJs—trained, anointed, and purpose-driven.

Mix with a purpose. Serve the King.

www.kingdomdjacademy.com

www.ingramcontent.com/pod-product-compliance
Lightning Source LLC
LaVergne TN
LVHW050937080826
845145LV00004B/1301

* 9 7 8 1 0 6 7 4 2 7 7 0 2 *